TAXIDERM~

A Historical Guide

CHAPTER I

TOOLS AND MATERIALS

The art of taxidermy, with its many methods of application, has furnished subject-matter for numerous books, most of these treating the subject in exhaustive style, being written primarily for students who desire to take up the work as a profession. It is the present author's purpose to set forth herein a series of practical methods suited to the needs of the sportsman-amateur who desires personally to preserve trophies and specimens taken on days spent afield with gun or rod.

The lover of field and gun may spend many fascinating hours at his bench, preparing, setting up, and finishing specimens of his own taking. Besides, the pursuit of this art will afford an amount of remuneration to the amateur who takes it up in a commercial way, doing work for others who have neither the time nor{10} inclination for preparing their own specimens.

The chief requisites for the beginner in taxidermy are joy in working out detail and a moderate amount of patience.

As suitable tools are the primary consideration in contemplating any work in taxidermy, a simple list follows. In this list no heavier work than the mounting of a Virginia deer head is dealt with. This outfit will be found practical for general light use:

A pocket-knife, one or two small scalpels, a kitchen paring-knife, an oil stone and can of oil, a hand drill, a fine fur-comb, one bone scraper, one small skin-scraper, one pair tinners' shears, one pair five and one-half inch diagonal wire cutters, one pair (same length) Bernard combination wire cutter and pliers, one pair small scissors, two or three assorted flat files, one hollow handle tool

1

holder with tools and little saw, one good hand-saw, one hack-saw, one upholsterer's regulator, one pair fine tweezers (such as jewelers use), one claw hammer, an assortment of round and furriers' needles, one or two darning needles, a sack needle, and an assortment of artists' small bristle and sable brushes (both round and flat).

Make your own stuffing rods, out of any size {11} iron wire, by hammering flat one end of a suitable length, filing teeth into the flat face thus made, and then bending a loop handle on the other end. This type of rod is easily curved or straightened to suit every need.

Those not wishing to buy at once the complete outfit named above will find that they can do good small work to start on with the aid of a pocket-knife, a pair of scissors, a pair of Bernard combination wire cutter and pliers, needles and thread, cord, a pair of tweezers, a hammer and saw, and small drill set.

Suitable materials follow the tools in order.

Arsenic is needed for the preservation of all specimens against moths. This is most effective when used in solution, which is made as follows: First dampen the arsenic powder with alcohol to saturate it quickly, when water is added. Place the arsenic in a large metal pail and to one-half pound of the powder add two gallons of water. Boil hard and steady over a good fire until the arsenic is completely dissolved. Place the solution thus made in an earthenware jar with closed cover, plainly marked "Poison," and keep out of reach of children. Allow solution to cool before applying to skins. Do not use the pail that the solution was made in for anything else. {12}

When using arsenic-water grease your hands with a little tallow, rubbing well under and around finger-nails and wiping the hands partially dry so that none of the grease will soil fur or feathers. This precaution will keep the arsenic from entering your skin.

Wash the hands with soap powder and a nail brush after work.

Apply arsenic-water with a brush, or a cotton-and-wire swab, to all inner surfaces of specimen skins.

Carbolic acid (best to procure U. S. P. pure crystals if possible) is needed for use in dilute form for relaxing dried skins. This prevents decay and does not injure the specimen skin. A few drops of the dissolved crystal to a quart of water is sufficient. Keep carefully labeled and in a safe place.

Following is a list of the materials needed for general light work:

A quantity of fine excelsior, fine tow and cotton batting, a quantity of various sizes of galvanized soft steel wire, an assortment of colored, enameled artificial eyes (procure a taxidermist's supply-house catalog and from this order your special tools and sizes and colors of eyes needed), a jar of liquid cement, dry glue (for melting up for papier-mache),{13} dry paper pulp, plaster of paris, Venetian turpentine, boiled linseed oil, boracic acid, some refined beeswax, a little balsam-fir, white varnish, turpentine, alcohol, benzine and a student's palette of tube oil colors (such as vermilion, rose madder, burnt sienna, yellow ochre, cadmium yellow middle, zinc white, cobalt blue, French ultramarine Blue, and Viridian).

Plastic compositions of papier-mache are essential, especially in mammal and game-head work, for properly finishing the details of ears, face, and feet of specimens after the body has been filled. These are applied partly as a last detail before mounting and partly after the figure is set up.

Compo. No. I is practical for all-around use. Take one-third hot melted glue and two-thirds flour paste (thick and thoroughly cooked). To this add a little boracic acid, a little arsenic powder, a very little of Venetian turpentine, a quantity of gray building-paper pulp (soak paper and squeeze and beat up even and then squeeze water out). To furnish a body to this mass, stir in dry white lead until middling thick. Beat the whole well together.

When carried so far this compo. is a powerful adhesive medium and may be employed to {14} stick tanned deer scalps to mannikins, and ear skin of same to the lead cartilages.

Compo. No. II is No. I with fine plaster of paris added until of the consistency of modeling clay or a trifle stiffer. This makes it ready for filling ear butts, eye sockets, noses, and feet for modeling into permanent shape. Sets by drying.

Compo. No. III is for monkey faces, vulture heads, lizards, turtles, etc. This composition dries very slowly and must be touched up now and then while drying, to preserve the details without warping. When dry it is like stone and holds the skin firmly. Take gray paper-pulp, hot melted glue (quantity according to amount of compo. needed), a little boracic acid (to prevent decay of glue), boiled linseed oil (fifty per cent. less than glue), a little arsenic powder (to prevent dermestes from eating into work), and to this mass add whiting until desired stiffness for modeling under skin is obtained. Beat and rub to an even smoothness and stop adding whiting at point where compo. is thick but still very sticky. Rub some of the compo. into inner surface of skin to be finished with it or skin will not take hold of mannikin or compo. to stay.

After modeling is finished under the skin {15} apply linseed oil on outside and repeat this application several times during the period

4

of drying. Watch and remodel details if any distortion attends the drying process.

Fine fleshy wrinkles and skin details can be worked out with this compo. It will hold a thin raw skin where it is put, but is not practical under fur or feathers.

Compo. No. IV may be used with wire netting or rough board as a base for making earth bases, imitation rock stands, etc. Take one-third hot melted glue, two-thirds flour paste, a quantity of paper pulp, a small amount of boiled linseed oil, a very little of Venetian turpentine, boracic acid, and arsenic. Thicken to modeling consistency with plaster of paris, coloring by adding some dry raw umber or lamp black and burnt umber.

Surface the bases made of this compo. by pressing sand, gravel, or forest mold into the face and when dry shake off the loose material. Touch up with tube colors, as desired, and when this is dry apply a very thin varnish and turpentine finish to bring out a natural damp look.

A foreword as to care of mountable specimens in the field may save a great amount of cleaning of mussed skins in the shop. {16}

All shot or bullet holes should be immediately plugged with cotton when specimens are taken. Take a little cotton along in your hunting coat for this purpose.

In birds plug also the mouth, nostrils, and vent to prevent escape of juices into plumage. A small sharpened twig will serve to place the plugs. Slip the bird head first into a paper cone for carrying.

Mussed or blood-stained specimens should not necessarily be discarded. Look them over first. Many such specimens may be cleaned very easily and come out in the finish as nearly perfect as others that appeared much better at the start.

{17}

PREPARING AND MOUNTING A BIRD

{19}

CHAPTER II

PREPARING AND MOUNTING A BIRD

With tools and materials assembled and table in readiness, we come to the real work and, in the order of things, will address the preparing and mounting of a fresh bird specimen. To many people

7

of long experience in the art of taxidermy this task never ceases to be a delightful operation, one of the pleasantest of many interesting bits of work that may result from a day spent afield.

Figuratively, the specimen lies before us, upon the bench. Make it any native bird your fancy desires. The following notes will be found to cover the ground:

A pencil and a sheet of wrapping paper will first be brought into service. With these make outlines of the specimen, top and side views, laying the bird upon the paper and drawing the pencil around it while looking straight down upon it.

After the skinning, outline the body, top, and side views, upon same sheet, with position[20] of shoulder joint, hip joint, knee, and tail marked in black spots.

This system of wrapping paper sketches will be found of great value in all work, from mounting a bird to setting up a deer head.

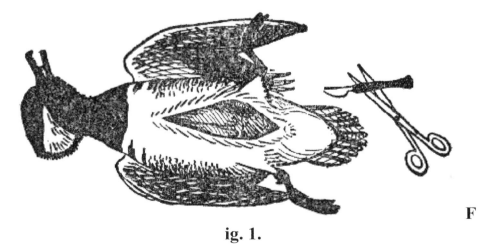

F

ig. 1.

To begin skinning, lay the bird upon a newspaper, head to left of you, on the bench. Have cornmeal handy. Part the belly and breast feathers up middle. With a scalpel make an incision (see Fig. 1) from within one inch of front end of breast bone back to a quarter-inch forward of the vent in large birds, and to the vent in small ones. Use care not to cut through abdominal wall, which is usually very thin and may easily be confused as a part of the skin, being closely bound to it. The two are easily separated, however.

The primary incision made, lift an edge of the skin with finger and thumb nail and carefully{21} tear skin free from body, using scalpel when necessary to help.

When thigh of a leg is exposed, take hold of leg outside of skin and push knee forward so it is uncovered inside of skin. Sever knee joint with scalpel or scissors, using care not to cut through skin on outside of joint. Repeat on other leg. Apply cornmeal or fine sawdust if blood or juice starts.

Next set bird on end, tail up. Bend tail over backward and cut through vent lining, tail muscles, and vertebrae forward of the large quills. Use care not to cut skin around tail, as at knee.

With bird still held on end, start peeling skin down over back and sides. Use scalpel if skin adheres tightly.

When pelvis is uncovered, if a small bird, take rump between two forefingers and thumb of left hand; if a large bird, hang up on a wire hook and cord, and skin down to shoulders.

Press wings forward strongly to loosen joint muscles. Cut through one shoulder joint and then other, going carefully as at knee and tail, so as not to cut skin on opposite side.

Plug with cotton or dry with meal wherever necessary to stop flowing blood.{22}

Next peel the neck skin down over head to bill, pulling out ear linings when met with and using care to work close to skull when cutting eyelids free.

When this is done, cut off base of skull. With this the skin is free from the body and inside out.

If the specimen is of a species with neck skin too small to peel over the head, turn head and neck back right side out when neck is only partly skinned down. Make an incision from middle of back of head down nearly half length of neck, alongside where nape is bare of feathers. Through this incision turn and clean the head.

With the skin removed, turn attention to details of cleaning away leg, wing, and tail muscles, removing eyes, brain, and jaw muscles from skull and scraping out whatever fat is in the skin.

To clean leg bones, skin out the thick, meaty shins, using thumb nail and scalpel to aid where necessary, down to heel joint or upper end of tarsus. Just above this joint sever the tendons, front and back, and peel leg muscles off.

In owls skin on down the tarsus to as near foot, or toes, as possible and clean out tarsus muscles.{23}

In large birds, next split ball of foot, insert point of a steel spindle under base of tarsus tendons beside hind toe and draw these cords out. This will sometimes require a strong pull.

Always do this after the leg above has been cleaned. In small birds it is not necessary to split ball of foot nor to remove these tendons.

Next remove the wing muscles. Peel skin down to elbow. Cut tendons free just above elbow and strip muscles off. To clean forearm in a small bird, use the thumb nail to shove skin forward toward wrist, on front of wing, without breaking union of large, secondary flight feathers with wing bone.

With scalpel cut and lift out elbow ends of forearm muscles, strip them out down to as near wrist as possible and cut off.

In a large bird, split skin of forearm and hand along under side after carefully separating feathers over bare strips of skin. Peel skin back both ways and remove flesh neatly. Scrape out whatever flesh is in evidence on hand bones in same way. In a bird with no fat adhering to the skin, the skull and tail only remain to be cleaned in order to complete the skinning operation.

To clean skull, remove eyes with a scalpel, scrape brains out through cut-off skull base,{24} and trim away jaw muscles and a portion of roof of mouth.

To clean tail, peel it out carefully and scrape and cut away fat and meat adhering to bone and base of quills.

If you have a specimen with fat adhering to the skin in more or less loose patches, as in hawks and owls, simply scrape or peel the fat off with a knife and thumb and finger.

If a fat duck skin is to be prepared the inside layer of skin over the fat tracts must be sheared off carefully with scissors and the fat then removed with a skin scraper or dull knife blade, care being exercised not to tear the outer skin or to pull through feathers with the grease.

To clean and degrease a bird skin which requires such treatment to prepare for mounting, wash it first in lukewarm ammonia water with mild soap. Squeeze from this washing and put through a bath of half-and-half alcohol and spirits of turpentine. Squeeze from this thoroughly and run through benzine. Compress and relax the skin repeatedly while immersed in both these baths. When squeezed from the benzine, dry the plumage by first burying the skin for some minutes in dry plaster of paris.

When nearly all the moisture is drawn out dust skin in the plaster until natural fluffiness is{25} restored. Do this last out of doors, where the skin may be beaten well when thoroughly dry, to free it of plaster dust. Lay skin, right side out, over the left hand and beat with the right, giving an occasional shaking, the better to loosen plaster dust.

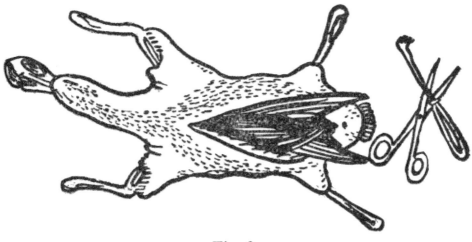

Fig. 2.

An A1 duster may be made from the brush of an ox tail. Nail this on a short piece of broomstick and square ends of hair with scissors. This duster is used instead of beating the plumage with the hand and does the work much quicker and better. When the dusting is done turn the skin inside out again (see Fig. 2) and brush arsenic-water into all inner surfaces, then turn skin right side out and brush a little of the solution upon the feet, under side of wings, and inside the bill.{26}

When poisoning the head, with skin inside out, one step in preparation for mounting is to be taken. After the arsenic-water is applied to skull and scalp, fill eye sockets with chopped tow or fine excelsior, put a light layer of cotton smoothly around the skull, forward edge close down to bill. Turn skin carefully back over skull and finish poisoning skin.

It is best, if possible to do without risk of decay, to fold the freshly prepared skin in a clean paper, wrap in damp cloth, and lay over one night in a cool place, before mounting. This allows arsenic-water to penetrate through into base of plumage, thus becoming more effective against moths than if skin were immediately filled with absorbent material which would tend to draw out the freshly applied solution.

With the skin preparation completed, construction of an artificial body is the next step. In all bird work, upholstery excelsior or "wood wool" will be found most satisfactory for body making and neck, wing, and leg wrapping. This may be found at almost any upholstery shop, as is also tow, a fine grade of which is needed in making bird necks, as chopped, soft filling, etc.

A good grade of long-fiber cotton is needed{27} for wrapping skulls and wing and leg bones in small birds, etc.

Various sizes of strong thread, both black and white, and some small, strong, ball twine will be needed for wrapping and sewing.

When making the artificial body, lay the outline sketches before you and copy Nature's lines throughout the work of assembling the specimen.

To make a firm core for the body, take a thick wisp of excelsior twice the length of the natural body and small or large according to specimen. Hold this tightly in the left hand, wrapping it very hard with thread or cord. Wrap the squeezed excelsior where it protrudes from between thumb and forefinger of left hand, drawing cord tight at each round, paying out the wisp until all is wrapped hard (see Fig. 3).

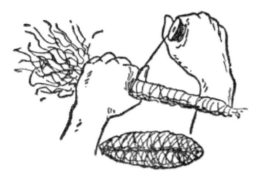

Fig. 3.

Now double this "stick" of excelsior in the {28} middle and bind it together tightly. This forms a solid core the length of the body.

The body is finished around this base by firmly binding upon it wisps or handfuls of loose excelsior until the shape of the natural body is approximated. To be correct this form should appear oval from side view and pear-shaped from end view (see Fig. 4).

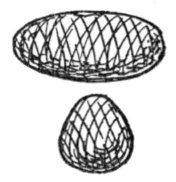

Fig. 4.

All body wrapping must be firm so that wires set in it will not be loose and cause the specimen to wobble.

Next cut the neck, wing, and leg wires. Cut neck wire three times natural length, wing wires twice natural length, and leg wires three times natural length. In the neck use a size wire that will support the head firmly and still be easy to manipulate.

If the wings are to be closed, use light wire in them. If to be spread, use strong wire to support with no wobbling. In the legs use as large wire as will go easily through the tarsus{29} and not rip the skin open, to insure rigidity in the finished specimen. Use galvanized soft steel wires if possible. If ordinary black iron wire is used it should be waxed before placing. For the tail cut one wire of a length to go half way through the body and leave enough protruding to allow of handily setting tail into position.

Cut six or eight medium wires, twice length of thickness of body, for wing pinning and feather wrapping, if either or both of these are found necessary. Make cornered points on wires. Sharpen neck- and wing-wires at both ends, leg, tail, and pinning-wires at one end.

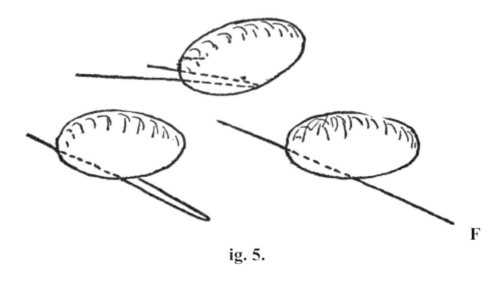

ig. 5.

To set neck-wire in body, thrust it in a little above center of larger end of body, run it diagonally through and out at middle back (see Fig. 5). Push two-thirds its length out of{30} back, loop one-third back along its own length and push it back through body so that both ends protrude, shorter end beneath other in front. Bend the short end squarely and force it into front of body to anchor neck-wire firmly in place. Consult note sketch and wrap a soft neck of natural size upon the wire (see Fig. 6). Leave head end of neck a little bit long to set into brain cavity for solid anchorage. For neck material use cotton in small birds, tow in medium size, and fine excelsior in large birds. Only excelsior will need tying down with thread or cord.

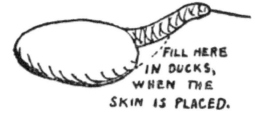

FILL HERE IN DUCKS, WHEN THE SKIN IS PLACED.

Fig. 6.

To make cords in nape of neck, which support the mane, thread a large sewing needle with heavy thread for small birds, a darning needle with string for larger. Double the cord and knot its end heavily. Run the needle through ridge of body just back of shoulders, carry cord to a little below where skull will set to and run cord through neck from back to front so it will protrude between jaws when they are set (see Fig. 7).{31}

Fig. 7.

Let long end of cord hang free so that it may be passed through the mouth when skull is set on neck-wire. With this done, lay aside the body.

DETAIL OF CLINCHING WIRE TIP.

WIRE DRAWN HEAVY TO SHOW PLAINLY.

Fig. 8.

The next step is wiring the wings and legs and substituting muscles of same. To place a wing-wire draw the wing inside out. Take wing bone in left hand. Place point of wire under small tendon that draws across back of elbow joint, push through and up to wrist. Turn wing right side out and by parting feathers on under side of wrist, locate two points of bone at joint which have a cord or tendon drawn{32} across between them. Work the wire through under this.

The simplest way to anchor tip of wing-wire is to push it outside skin just forward of wrist, turn a short right angle bend near its tip with pliers and carrying it forward, push the point through a hollow pan which will be found in the hand bones (see Fig. 8).

After a wing-wire is set, wrap cotton, tow, or excelsior about the upper arm-bone to approximate shape and size of flesh removed. Wrap slightly with thread or cord and tie.

In a small bird in which the forearm was skinned out from the inside, slip in a film of cotton or tow to replace flesh of same. In a large bird in which the wing was opened along forearm and hand, lay in a soft filling after skin is in place on artificial body and sewn up. Sew wing incision carefully, beginning at body and keeping feathers out of stitch.

To place the leg-wires, start sharpened end into ball of foot, push wire upward through back of leg to hock or heel joint. Take leg in left hand, keeping heel straight, and push wire through at back of joint. A little turning of the wire will aid in passing through leg easily.

Now turn leg inside out and push wire to just beyond end of shin bone (see Fig. 9).{33} Slip wire rapidly back and forth in leg to make it run easily. There should be no kinks in wires.

Fig. 9.

Hold wire down to back of bone and wrap on cotton, tow, or excelsior, according to size of bird, to replace flesh. Tie this material loosely with a few turns of thread or cord. See that wing and leg wrapping is smooth and nicely tapering from elbow and heel.

It now remains to place the body, set wings and legs and tail, sew up the breast incision, and, if a large bird, the wings.

In preparing to place the body, take a turn of end of nape cord about tip of neck-wire and twist a wisp of cotton about them both to prevent wire catching in neck skin when passing through. Hold up the bird-skin by the head, shake it out loose and rattle neck-wire up through the neck. Run wire out of mouth, remove cotton and release free end of nape cord. Draw wire back to base of skull, leaving nape cord hanging from mouth. Now push wire{34} through brain cavity, between eye sockets and forward out of roof of mouth inside until neck is seated in brain cavity. Tip of wire may have to be curved to accomplish this, in curve-billed birds.

When head is set take excelsior body in right hand, hold it with head up, and with left hand pull shoulder skin into place. Now lay the bird down, take a wing-wire and start it through the body at side of back, one-half to one and one-half inches, according to size of bird, to rear of actual position of shoulder joint.

Pull wire through on opposite side of breast. When head of wing-bone is drawn down to same distance as above, from body, bend wire sharply forward to lay upon body, thus setting shoulder joint so that it is flexible. Now turn over end of wire left protruding from side of breast and clinch it into body squarely. When wings are set shake skin down over body and set legs.

Having previously marked the hip joint with a spot of ink, run a leg-wire through at this point, quartering it out on opposite side where thigh will set. Pull wire through to a considerable length without drawing other end up into the foot. {35}

Loop sharp end squarely, with long enough point to go clear through body again, push it back through, clinching tip down on other side. Now pull the knee to its proper distance from hip joint, thus leaving bare wire for thigh bone. Bend thigh into place flat against side of body, with knee at side of breast.

When legs are set shake and carefully pull skin of rump into place. Take tail-wire and push it through center of tail, under the bone, using care that it does not disturb tail quills. Push sharp end of wire into body above center and forward of end of body.

Consult notes for actual set of tail. See that wire supports tail without looseness. (For general details of wiring, see Fig. 10.) Fill butt of tail and thighs with a little chopped tow.

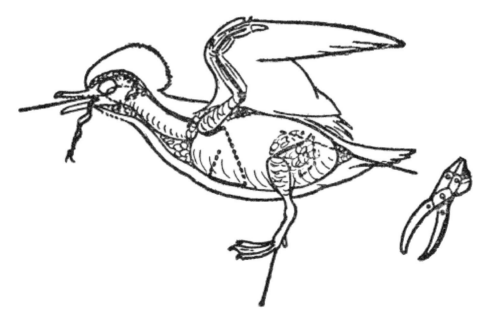

Fig. 10.

{36}

Now lay the bird upon its back. Turn the legs out at the sides a little, leaving knees against body. Draw edges of skin together along incision and sew up with medium stitches, neither short and labored or long and slouchy. Begin at rump end of incision.

In a bird in which the neck was opened to accommodate skinning the head, sew up this incision carefully, beginning at body end and sewing toward head.

When a large bird, in which the wings were opened for cleaning, is to be mounted with closed wings, very little sewing need be done, but if the wings are to be raised or spread the incision should be neatly stitched its entire length.

Also in a large bird, in which the tendons were drawn through ball of foot, the fatty tissue of the ball should be replaced with chopped tow and the short incision sewn up. Beeswax will keep thread from fraying.

With the sewing all done, bend the legs into semi-position, fold the wings, if to be closed, and turn them sharply up over the back so that their under side is outward and elbows meet over center of back. Shake out the plumage a little by grasping the feet. Drill the perch and mount the bird upon it. Position the legs, body,{37} and head, and set the tail as per Nature, to suit the position.

Adjust the plumage a little with tweezers. Compress the wings loosely to the sides. If there is an unnatural hollowness between the shoulders, lift the mane and at one side of it where the skin is bare, make a short longitudinal incision. Through this place a little soft filling over and between the shoulders to fill out hollowness. It is not necessary to sew up this incision in a long feathered specimen.

Now settle down to the fascinating task of adjusting the feather tracts, nicely manipulating the plumage, in places feather by feather, until characteristic markings of the species are brought out in their normal position as though the bird had just ruffled and then allowed the feathers to settle back softly. Jewelers' tweezers are the finest thing to be had for this work.

Return to the head. Pull the nape cord taut and tie it to neck-wire in roof of mouth. Cut off the wire within the mouth so that the mandibles close naturally. Tie the bill shut with cord or thread. It is necessary in many specimens to thread the cord through the nostrils to accomplish this.

To set the eyes, wipe a drop of liquid glue into the cotton of the eye sockets and inside the{38} lids, using a bit of wire for the purpose. Set the eyes with regard to expression to suit the position, picking the lids over their edges with needle and tweezers.

Pin, or tie with thread, the toes to grasp the perch.

Cut two pieces of thin cardboard for the tail. Curve them slightly. Place one over and one under the long quills just clear of the coverts and pin them through in two or three places to hold the quills even until dry.

In mounting a specimen with spread wings, card the flight feathers full length with curved strips, same as tail, then run a long sharpened wire into the body under each wing and lay a loose bunch of cotton over it, under the quills, to raise them and hold in proper position until dry.

To wrap the body feathers for keeping place until dry, stick two or three long pins in back and breast, along center of both. These hold the light wrapping of thread from slipping out of place as it goes on. Lay the thread around the specimen lightly. If the wings do not set right without other aid than the wire already in them, pin them with sharpened wires, one through the double bone just forward of the wrist and one through close forward of the elbow,{39} running wires firmly into the body. (For general details see Fig. 11.)

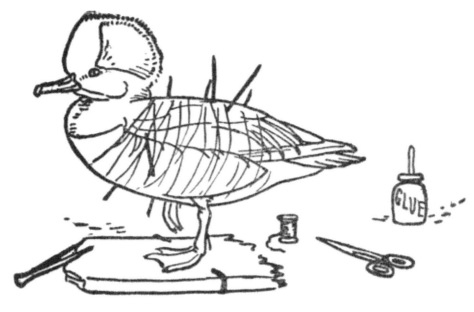

Fig. 11.

To soak up a dried bird skin for preparation to mount, the simplest and quickest means is immersion in a weak solution of carbolic acid in water, leaving for a day or two until tissues are soft.

When the skin is relaxed so that wings and legs may be manipulated without breaking, squeeze water from it and follow same method given for cleaning a fresh skin. With this treatment a good dry skin will come out as soft and workable as a fresh one. Arsenic and grease burnt skins are hard to get much out of.

To make up dry bird skins for keeping to {40} mount at a future time, follow regular method of thorough skinning and cleaning. Apply dry arsenic powder to inner surfaces. Wrap skull, wing, and leg bones lightly with cotton or tow. Turn skin right side out and push a neck and light body filling of fiber that will allow ventilation, into place. Arrange the plumage and hang the skin up by a thread or cord sewn through neck at base of skull.

To make a cabinet skin for study purposes, roll a neat body and neck of material to suit size of bird, place it inside the skin, stitch incision together, plug eye sockets with cotton, tie the elbows together on the body with a loop sewn through the back, tie bill shut, adjust feathers neatly and lay the specimen in a hollowed bed made of a piece of wire netting bent to size. See that wings cover back neatly. Lay head of short necked bird out straight, neck somewhat shorter than natural, and of long necked specimen along right side, looped to body with cord sewn through neck and side. Cross the feet and tie with a tag bearing complete data as to locality, date, sex, etc., with collector's name. To determine sex of a bird specimen, open the abdomen under thigh. Testes of male will be found under fore end of pelvis and are white, in young bird, very small. {41}

Now when the period of drying is past, return to the mounted bird for finishing touches. With scissors cut the thread feather wrappings. Pull out pins in back and breast and cut off wing pinning-wires flush under the plumage. If the specimen was primarily mounted on a rough temporary perch, remove to the finished permanent stand and color legs and fleshy, exposed parts of face skin to natural hues with tube oil colors and a soft brush. Thin the color for this purpose with a little turpentine and a very little touch of varnish.

In all work in taxidermy, practice develops deftness and a personal system of handling the details that cannot be brought about except by sympathetic attention to the art. The work is not difficult when the details are addressed with quiet thought and very little main strength.

{43}

SKINNING, PREPARING, AND MOUNTING A SMALL MAMMAL

{45}

CHAPTER III

SKINNING, PREPARING, AND MOUNTING A SMALL MAMMAL

We will choose a gray squirrel as our subject in this chapter, as this little rodent has a tough skin that is easily manipulated. A cottontail rabbit might be more easy to procure, but is not so satisfactory for the purpose of initiative steps in this work, as his skin is extremely delicate and requires especially careful handling in preparation and mounting.

Now, in beginning work upon the small mammal specimen, make outline studies of it in same way the bird specimen was handled, *i. e.*, both before and after skinning. When the preliminary surface sketches are completed, replace the wrapping paper used for the purpose, with newspaper, cornmeal at hand, and proceed with the skinning.

Have scalpel or skinning-knife well sharpened. Lay head of specimen toward right. Part fur over center of breast bone, insert point of knife just under skin, forcing backward, {46} and with as near one clean stroke as possible open the skin neatly along center of abdomen. Do not cut the abdominal wall. Carry belly incision to close to the vent. In male specimen run the incision to one side of the testes.

Next insert point of knife in fore center of pad or feet and paws and with a gentle push carry these incisions upon back of wrists and inside of ankles to where swell of large muscles is felt. In mammals the size of woodchuck or raccoon, split toes on under side.

If a mammal skin is to be kept for some time, dried or in brine, split the tail full length along under side. If tail skin slips easily and the specimen is to be mounted at once, pull the tail out, splitting only the very tip to allow arsenic solution to be run through. In many species the tail must be split and peeled out with a knife because of tough binding. (For general diagram of incisions, see Fig. 12.)

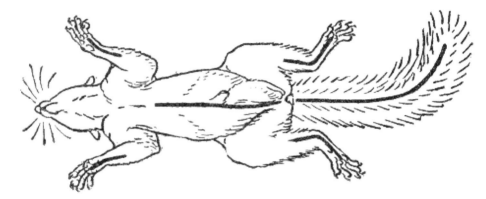

Fig. 12.

{47}

The next step in handily skinning a mammal is to peel out the feet through their incisions, severing toes at base and leaving them complete in the skin. Peel the leg skins back over ankles and wrists (see Fig. 13).

Fig. 13.

If tail was split, peel it down next, beginning at tip. Now return to the abdominal incision and neatly peel the skin from the body, in many instances using only the thumb nail for loosening it.

When the thighs are encountered, bend hind legs back and sever hip joints from pelvis (see Fig. 13), cutting carefully through the large muscles so that the skin on opposite side of them may not be punctured. {48}

When the hind legs are cut free, peel around back of pelvis, loosening skin to base of tail. Set the specimen upon its head end and, with thumb and finger nails of left hand, grasp skin about the base of tail while with right hand strip tail out with force.

Next peel the body down to shoulders. Hang large specimen up by cord tied about loins, the more handily to finish the skinning.

Sever the forelegs at shoulder joint (see Fig. 14), using care not to cut through skin.

Fig. 14.

Peel skin down over neck to ears. Cut ears free from head, working with knife close to skull. Peel to eyes. In cutting the eyelids free, work close to eyeballs so that lids are not injured. Peel to mouth and cut close to jaw bones in severing lips and nose from skull (see Fig. 15).

With the skin removed from the body, next peel out the legs. {49}

Split inside of lips free with sharp knife, very carefully, so as not to break edge of them.

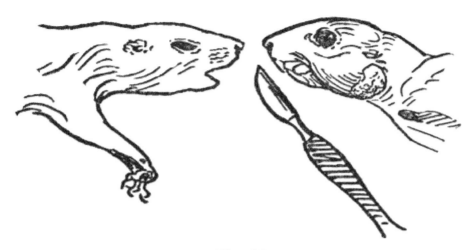

Fig. 15.

With scissors shear out all mouth and nose meat, being careful not to cut off the whisker pockets, which are usually very prominent when the side nose muscles are partly sheared off.

Skin out the backs of the ears clear to edges by pressing a finger tip inside the ear and peeling over this with finger nail or other dull instrument. With scissors shear off meat of butt of ear and whatever meat and fat adheres to rest of skin.

In sketches of skinned body mark points of shoulder joint and hip joint and note width of pelvis at hip joints.

Remove the skull from the carcass and clean it by cutting and scraping away all meat, pulling out the eyeballs, and scooping out the brain. {50} For the purpose of mounting, the base of the skull may be cut off to facilitate cleaning, but for study (cabinet) skins the skull must be kept intact and always accompany by number the skin it was removed from.

Trim all meat from the leg bones and poison these and the skull when finishing preparation of the skin.

30

Add a few drops of carbolic acid, well stirred in to the arsenic water used upon skins of small mammals for mounting. This aids in preventing decay and slipping of the epidermis.

Apply the poison solution thoroughly with a brush, to all inner surfaces of the skin and to the toes. If tail was split only at the tip, run a few drops of arsenic water through it.

Turn the poisoned skin right side out, lay it flat, side pressed to side, roll up, place in paper, and cover with a damp cloth. Lay in this way over one night, giving the arsenic solution a chance to penetrate through to roots of hair before mounting. If a specimen is bloody or mussed the blood may be cleaned off before skinning by wetting the spots with alcohol and rubbing the blood and juices out with cornmeal.

The first step in mounting is properly to wire the skull and leg bones. (For details of this see Fig. 16.){51}

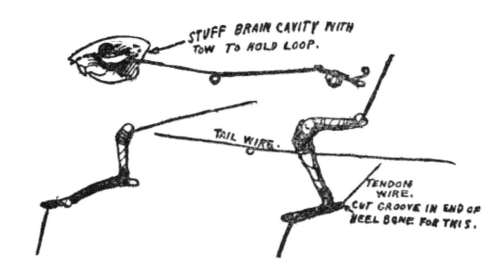

Fig. 16.

For the body-wire select a size larger than for the legs, cutting it twice as long as head, neck, and body. For legs choose a size wire that will firmly support the specimen in position without wobbling. If the mammal is to sit erect, the hind leg-wires must be considerably larger than otherwise and foreleg-wires may be much lighter. (Making the pelvis loop may be easily followed in diagram in Fig. 17.)

Fig. 17.

{52}

The first body-wire loop is bent to set into the brain cavity. Then the foreleg loop is made some little distance back of actual shoulder point (in fox-squirrel about an inch and a half or two inches). Get distance from skull to hip joint from body sketch and follow this sketch for dimensions in bending wire pelvis into shape. The tail loop is last to be made.

As Fig. 16 shows, the leg-wires are wrapped tightly upon the back of the bones with thread or light cord, leaving shorter end of wire passing from sole of foot. At shoulder joint turn wire back sharply and at hip ball turn wire in at right angles. In palms and soles of feet turn wire down at right angles.

When the bone wiring is completed take up again the body sketches. Bring out a quantity of fine excelsior for replacing the leg muscles and skull meat and for filling the body after assembling the wired parts within the skin.

In wrapping on the artificial leg muscles begin at the feet. Follow the outline sketches and with thread and small cord wrap small, properly proportioned masses, squeezed firm in the hand or finger tips, upon the bones, copying Nature's outline and form accurately.

Wrap the foreleg to the shoulders. Complete the hind leg to the knee and above this{53} point wrap on only the muscles on top of the thigh bone, leaving back of thigh to be filled with loose material when the skin is adjusted.

The tail may be made of cotton, wrapped tightly and smoothly upon the wire, wisp by wisp. Begin at tip and work down, spinning the wire with right hand to produce uniformity of shape. If mammal is larger than a squirrel the tail may be made of tow, pulled smooth, laid lengthwise of the wire, and wrapped smoothly down with thread. For size, length, and shape of tail, refer to the sketches.

The head muscles may be replaced in much the same manner as leg muscles. (See Fig. 18 for wrapping complete.) The specimen is now ready to assemble.

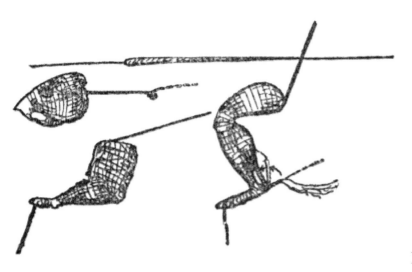

Fig. 18.

To accomplish this in systematic order, insert the head into place and next the forelegs.{54} Consult sketch and bend a right angle in foreleg-wire back of shoulder at such a point that shoulder will set in proper relation to head. One at a time, using the pliers, twist these foreleg-wire ends, after setting them through shoulder loop, tightly back along the body-wire. Next insert the hind legs into the skin. Slip their wires through hip loops, carry them forward, and tightly twist them around body-wire as in forelegs.

If the tail skin was unopened except at tip the wrapped tail should be put in when the head is placed in the skin. If tail skin was opened full length, the artificial tail may be placed after all the legs are adjusted. Run tail-wire base forward through its pelvis-wire loop and twist it around body-wire. (For general assembling of specimen see Fig. 19.)

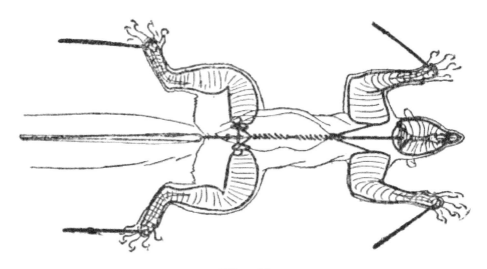

Fig. 19.

{55}

Before filling the body, sew up the tail, using short stitches and a round needle, if it is possible to push it through skin easily. Begin sewing at tip and work toward body. Finish all sewing with a simple knot drawn tight under tip of finger.

Next, with a stuffing rod of appropriate size, place the neck filling, stuffing against palm of left hand hollowed outside the skin at point of filling so that the forming may be felt accurately.

Then comes the filling for shoulder blades over forelegs and with it the chest filling. In handling the excelsior, pull out wisps of it from the mass and rub them between the palms so that the fiber is broken up and softened. Fine excelsior ("wood wool") is the material par excellence for stuffing the bodies of small mammals from size of small chipmunks up. Mice require a softer material, and short chopped, fine tow answers requirements in them. The leg bones of mice may be wrapped with long fiber cotton batting or fine tow.

When the shoulders and chest have been filled firm full, but not to the point of looking stuffed, turn to the hind legs and pelvis. Fill in the back thigh muscles neatly; then cover top of wire pelvis, pushing material well down to{56} base of tail. Fill rump sufficiently to overcome a pinched or too high set look. The position must be considered in properly filling the back, sides, and abdomen. If a bunched up position is to be worked out, bend the wire back bone into semipose and place the legs in approximately their final position. After this, fill the body to suit the position, always forming with the stuffing rod working against the left hand. See that all filling is firm but not packed in to the point of distorting the skin. Consult sketches and aim to preserve the little animal's natural form. (For general filling details see Fig. 20)

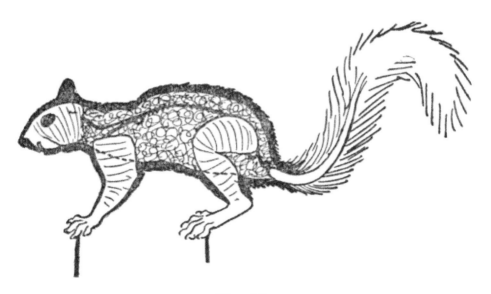

Fig. 20.

When the filling is all placed, sew the abdominal incision neatly up, beginning at rear end always and going forward. Wax the thread.{57} In a hunched together position, middling long stitches may be used. In a straighter pose shorter stitches should be used.

Now, when the body is sewn up cover the specimen with paper and a damp cloth to prevent drying while a small batch of compo. No. II is prepared for finishing feet and head. Returning to the specimen with this, slightly moisten the wrapping on the bones of the feet and apply a bit of the compo. at front and in the sole of each foot. This cements the toes to the foot and fills the pads.

After this is done sew each foot up neatly, beginning at toes and working toward body. If toes were large and required splitting and removing of toe cords, replace the cords with bits of small rope or soft twine and sew toes up neatly with short stitches. It is best to use a round needle and black thread, well waxed for this work.

The specimen is now ready to place upon its base, perch, or stand. With the approximate position shaped, mark the perch for wire holes by holding specimen over it and indicating places where wires come, by scratch or pencil mark. When holes are drilled and the specimen wired into place, take a strong fur needle set into a handle and by working and compressing{58} with the fingers and jab-lifting with the needle, finish shaping and positioning.

Hold in hollow of flanks by sewing through here with long needle and strong cord, heavily knotted for the first hold. Finish this sewing with a knot drawn down into the fur under the thumb. Arrange the fur over all stitches by picking it free with tweezers.

With the body finished, take up filling and finishing the head with the compo. First work compo. into the ears and pinch them out thin and into their natural shape, then cover the entire face under the skin with compo. Fill eye sockets and set eyes as second step.

Lastly fill the nose and lips and model them firmly upon the jaws. In all mammals cover the teeth well with the lips. Even in a muskrat the teeth do not ordinarily show at all. Also avoid getting the lips, nose, and whisker base too full. Set the tail into easy normal position, pin toes to grasp the perch or set well upon the ground and inspect the body to see that no hollow or bumps remain in the filling where there should be perfect smoothness. Remove such of these as persist with the handle-held fur needle and then set the specimen in a well ventilated place to dry.

The principal point in preparing thin or{59} stretchy small mammal skins for mounting is to leave the membrane of skin-muscles on the body skin. This holds a flabby skin in shape and lends strength to a frail one. In spite of this the legs of most wild rabbits must be handled very gingerly, as they have no lining membrane like the body. For finishing mouth, nose, and eyelids of mounted mammals, melt a little refined beeswax in a metal vessel. While the wax is hot (don't allow it to smoke), stir in a little tube oil color (black or brown for most mammals; color to nature for birds with highly tinted eyelids). Mix the wax and color thoroughly with a flat bristle brush. Afterward the brush may be easily cleaned of the wax by breaking it up with alcohol, when it has cooled.

Next draw some wisps of fine, long-fiber cotton through the melted wax and lay them quickly flat upon oiled paper to cool. For lips of mammals cut narrow strips of the wax. Heat an upholstering spindle and with it repeatedly heated, melt the wax and cotton into crease of closed lips. Melt thin, flat pieces of the wax into depth of nostrils and very narrow strips in eyelids.

When all the wax is placed, model it into shape with a smooth, wedge-ended bit of pine {60} wood. To clean out wax that ran into the hair by melting, apply alcohol with a bit of cloth, scratch the waxy hair loose with finger nail and rub the crumbled wax out with the bit of alcohol dampened cloth. This leaves lips, eyelids, and nostrils neatly finished. Apply thin varnish to nose, edge of eyelids, and bare parts of lips that show. For mounting a mammal with open mouth, follow same note given in making a whole head for rug.

To make a small mammal cabinet skin, remove the skin as for mounting except that legs are severed at elbow and knee and soles of feet are split only to allow of poisoning.

Poison with dry arsenic. Wire tail same as in mounting. Wrap leg bones with cotton, tow, or excelsior according to size of specimen. Turn the skin back over a core of one of these materials, wrapped upon a splinter or stick, to size of natural body, but somewhat flatter. Sew up abdominal incision neatly. Catch the lips together with two or three stitches. Lay specimen, belly down, upon a soft-wood board. Pin fore paws alongside of the face and hind feet alongside of tail.

When this is done press specimen until it is slightly flattened and set aside to dry. With each specimen preserve the perfect skull when{61} possible, date on which taken, locality, any note of interest observed at the time (and add collector's name).

In using dry arsenic, apply with a small brush, using no grease on the hands.

PREPARING AND MOUNTING GAME FISHES AND SMALL REPTILES

{65}

CHAPTER IV

PREPARING AND MOUNTING GAME FISHES AND SMALL REPTILES

For the purpose of mounting, fishes and reptiles must be fresh, and the fresher the better. In beginning this chapter it may be well to state a simple way to keep fish for a short period before skinning and mounting, as sportsmen afield will not always be able immediately to prepare specimens taken.

First, while the fish is perfectly fresh, remove the viscera. If the fish is to be mounted upon a panel for wall decoration, make the incision along middle of poorest looking side, full length from gill to tail fin.

If the specimen is to stand upon a pedestal of polished wood, with supporting rods from the belly, make the incision along center of belly full length. To prevent decay, stir three or four drops of forty per cent solution of formalin into a quart of water.

Squeeze a cloth from this, leaving it pretty moist, and wrap the fish in it, giving the wet{66} cloth close contact with the skin. Do not apply formalin inside any skin to be used for mounting. Never eat the flesh of a fish thus kept.

Before skinning the fish, make careful outlines over him, both side and top views. When skin is removed make outlines of skinned carcass.

Handle a fish very carefully when skinning and cleaning, moving the specimen about or bending as little as possible during the entire operation. Lay the head to your left. Open the skin with scissors and make one long clean cut.

Lift edges of the skin and peel from flesh with a sharp knife or scalpel. Cut off base of fins, when encountered, with scissors or bone snips. Trim out most of skull with knife and bone snips, removing eyes from inside. Be sure to scrape all flesh from cheek inside of gill cover.

Remove flesh and fat from inside of skin with scraper, working from tail toward head. Scrape out with point of small knife blade the flesh that runs out thin over tail-fin bones.

This completes the skinning operation. The cleaned skin may be poisoned to advantage with either dry or solution arsenic, brushed in well. {67}

If the specimen is opened on the side for panel mounting and we wish to follow a very simple method in mounting, one that is quite as practical as it is simple, we must take a different step than outline sketches before skinning. This is to make a complete body and head cast of the best side in plaster of paris. This does not include the fins. To make the cast neatly, lay the fish, best side up, in a slight hollow in a box of clean, damp sand. Pack the sand up under the fish body smoothly so that more than half of him rises in cameo style from the smooth surface.

Make up enough plaster to do the cast at once. To mix plaster properly, sprinkle it into the dish of water until a little will begin to stand out dry above the surface. Then with a spoon sunk deep in it, gently stir to evenness. It is then ready to pour. Before doing this, jar the pan upon the table a time or two to cause any possible bubbles to rise.

Pour evenly over the fish, or better still, dip it on with the spoon. The plaster should be thick enough to barely flow for making a proper cast.

The pectoral fins are simply laid flat to the side in making the cast.

Allow the cast to set hard before lifting it{68} and removing the fish. Trim off the overlapping edge so that no undercut remains.

The cleaned and poisoned skin should lay in damp cloth over one night and is then laid in accurate place back in the cast. Pour it nearly full of medium thick plaster of paris, carefully mixed free of bubbles.

Settle a board, cut to approximate body outline but much smaller, into the unset plaster and press the flap edges of the skin back together over the board, molding edge of back and belly to round back away from trimmed edge of mold. This must be all done with accuracy before the plaster sets, but you will find it gives enough time. Do not work in a strung-up, nervous way.

When the plaster is set hard, remove fish from mold, hold it upon palm of left hand and tack edges of skin to back-board. (For general details of this method see Fig. 21).

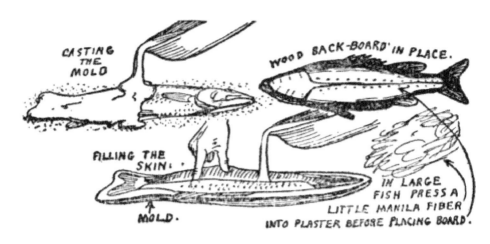

Fig. 21.

{69}

Screw the specimen to a piece of board and adjust fins, carding them over little blocks and holding the cards with sharp toilet pins until drying is completed.

See that the jaws set right. They should have gone into the mold in proper relation to each other. Dig out the plaster in eye socket on show side and set eye in a little fresh plaster.

A simple method of making a modelled mannikin for fish follows:

Have the freshly skinned body or sketches of same at hand. Cut a soft-wood board core, making it some smaller than outline of carcass.

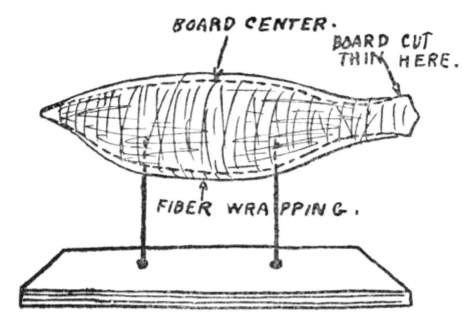

Fig. 22.

Anchor into this two rigid supporting wires or rods as shown in Fig. 22. Upon this board{70} core wrap strongly and smoothly with thread or small cord a quantity of manila fiber to same shape of body but one-half to three-quarters inch smaller than the body. Over this apply plaster of paris and manila fiber (dipping the fiber and laying it on) to approximate size of natural body. When this is set hard, pare it smoothly into outlines of natural shape and gouge out slight grooves for fin bases to set into. (See Fig. 23.).

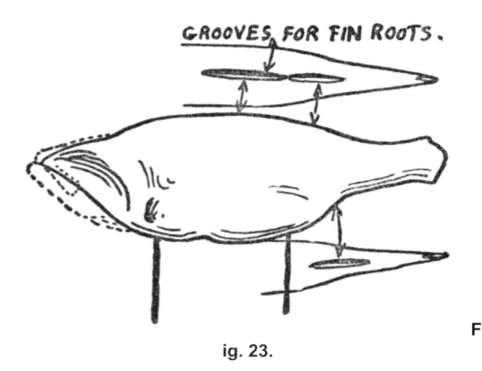

GROOVES FOR FIN ROOTS.

F

ig. 23.

Mannikins of this type should be dried out as quickly as possible and shellaced before applying the skin. Apply the fish skin with a paste of compo. No. I. Card the fins as in Fig. 24.

Fill the face through mouth and eyes with {71} plaster of paris with a little chopped manila fiber worked into it. Use a slight amount of glue in the water to prevent rapid setting of the plaster. Hold face in place until set, with light wrapping of soft cord, using care that it does not crease soft parts.

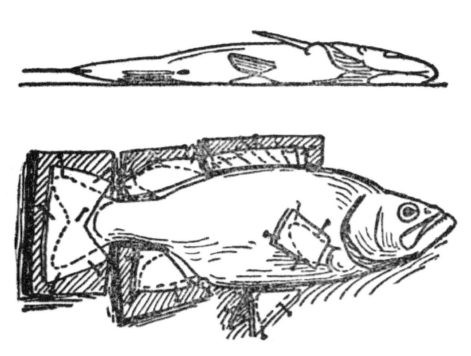

Fig. 24.

Special fish eyes may be procured at any dealers in taxidermists' supplies. As the last detail of mounting, set the eyes. In all kinds of specimens use a size of eyes that pass through the lids easily without the need of stretching to admit them. A panel-fish needs but one eye as a rule.

When the specimen is dry apply a coat of{72} thin shellac as a filler to the surface to paint upon. This filler should be very thin and leave only a suggestion of gloss.

Use oil colors and apply as little pigment as may be used for the effect. Kerosene oil is an ideal thinning medium for tube oil colors. Have very little paint upon the brush when applying the tints to a fish or reptile skin.

A suggestion of natural hues and markings will be found more satisfactory than painting them on heavily. In a day or two when the paint is dry apply a very thin coat of alcohol-cut picture varnish. Turps-cut varnish is liable to loosen the paint, thus necessitating entire re-finishing. Fasten a panel fish to the setting that is to frame him, with two screws at least, countersinking their heads in the panel back.

The fish piece may be hung as a picture, with screw eyes and cord or it may be hung with one or two sheet metal slots countersunk into the panel back. This will allow the piece to be applied flat to any wall that will hold screws.

Large fishes mounted with rods for pedestal setting should have rods threaded at both ends for nuts. Upper ends that support core board should be bent as shown in Fig. 25. This figure{73} also shows complete method of setting both rod and wire supports in body core and permanent stand.

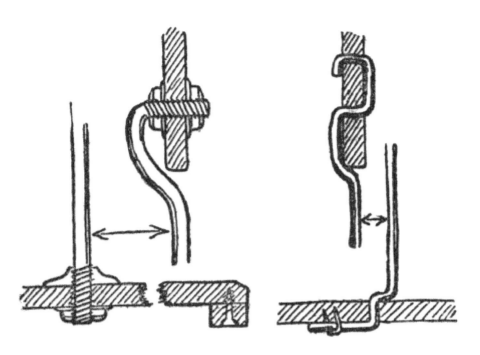

Fig. 25.

PREPARING AND MOUNTING A SMALL HARD SHELLED
TURTLE

For the purpose of skinning a hard shelled turtle (soft shelled species are best unattempted) the belly plate is sawed open as shown in Fig. 26. A piece of hacksaw blade may be shaped and set into a firm handle with cross pegs of metal, for this purpose, or the small saw found in a hollow handle tool kit may serve. Four corner holes must be bored by{74} which to start the sawing, which, for ease in accomplishing, may be thus done upon straight lines.

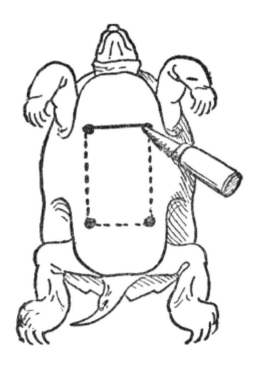

Fig. 26.

Through the sawed opening remove the viscera. With scissors and bone snips, free the legs at their joints with the back shell, cut the neck and tail vertebrae free and pull all these members inside out through the opened shell. Skin the head to well down behind the eye sockets, uncovering most of the jaw muscles and stopping where the skin and skull are joined directly on the crown.

Cut the neck off. Clean out jaw meat, tongue, and brain. Turn head right side out and with a stiff wire hook pull out the eyeballs.{75}

Skin legs clear to toes and remove flesh cleanly from bones.

Skin tail out carefully. In many species this has to be split on under side to remove bone. Dry the shell out with a bit of rag.

Poison well with arsenic water and let stand over one night, covered with a damp cloth.

A simple method of mounting turtles, that will be found satisfactory for decorative work, is clearly shown in Figs. 27 and 28.

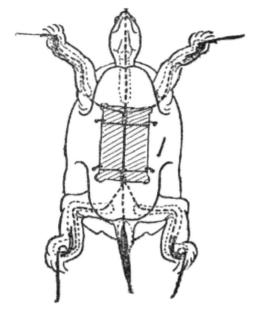

Fig. 27.

A light tow neck is wrapped upon the neck-wire, which is cut about twice the length of the head and neck-skin, and has a small loop bent into it near its outer end, to set into the brain cavity and a loop by front and one by back end{76} of belly opening to hold leg-wires. The front end is run out through the nose. Legs are wired as in a mammal with wires bound firmly to bones with thread or cord. Bones are then covered with a light wrapping of tow, placed lightly and smoothly. This serves only as a core to the filling. Tail is wrapped upon wire to natural size.

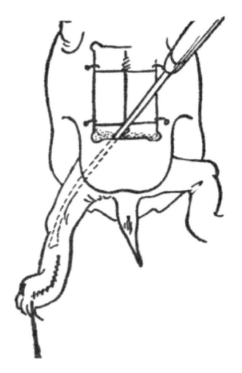

Fig. 28.

Legs are now pushed back into place, wires of them and tail are passed through loops in body-wire and twisted around it once or twice, and then leg-wires are led to drilled holes in edge of shell and clinched in them as shown in Fig. 27.{77}

Now tie or pin the mouth shut. Legs and head and neck are next filled with sawdust, tamped in with a blunt piece of rod or wire or piece of wood shaped for the purpose. Fill in the front legs and head first and stuff some tow behind them to hold the sawdust in place when the specimen is reversed to fill hind legs. After these are filled, stuff the shell full of tow.

Position the turtle and wire upon a piece of board for a temporary base.

Finish shaping with a whittled modeling tool. Stuff the skin in front of hind legs into proper concavity with wads of tow or cotton and leave these until the specimen is dried.

Stuff the eye sockets with chopped tow. Wipe inside the eyelids a little liquid glue and carefully set the eyes, using care to preserve natural fullness of the ball under lids.

In drying, the tip of the nose will shrink away. When the specimen is dry and the nose-wire is cut off, a wax tip may be modeled on, nostrils being punched into it with a bit of wire.

To set the wax nose, with a sharp knife trim away the shrunken tip, place a bit of wax upon the socket, and melt it into firm contact with a heated wire. Shape the artificial nose with a small wooden modeling tool. Replace faded{78} colors of turtles with thin tints of tube colors.

An ideal method of mounting turtles is to finish head, neck, legs, and tail in compo. No. II.

Use the leg bones and wrap them thinly with tow. Wrap a small, hard, tow neck upon the wire and a thin tow core upon the tail-wire. Cover these cores, to natural size of muscles, with papier mache.

Cover the skull where meat was scraped from jaws. Push the neck, tail and legs into place and wire to shell as in Fig. 27. Stuff shell with tow to hold papier mache filling of limbs in place until dry.

Turtles mounted in this way should be positioned upon a board, modeled with a tool into anatomical lines of neck, legs, etc., and allowed to remain wired upon the board until the compo. begins to harden.

When this is well under way, take the turtle from the board and finish drying, wrong side up in a well ventilated place. Remove the tow from inside the shell to allow of quicker evaporation. Turtles mounted with sawdust dry very quickly and usually very slowly when finished in papier mache.

PREPARING AND MOUNTING A SMALL LIZARD

(Apply the wrapped body principle, given herewith, to mounting small snakes, using a wire through center.)

{79}

A horned toad is a good example for us to work out in this department. Skin the specimen as you would a small mammal, except that body incision runs from jaw to tip of tail and skull is left attached to face-skin. Keep the skinned carcass in alcohol for reference in making the hard wrapped excelsior body. Mount as you would a bird specimen, except that all leg-wires are set solid same as the two legs of the bird are.

The lizard's leg bones are wired exactly as in a bird and are wrapped with tow or cotton to replace muscles. Wire neck and tail and put the specimen together as shown in Fig. 29.

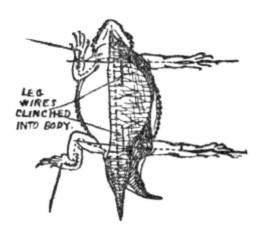

Fig. 29.

Position the specimen and wire upon a temporary base. Set eyes same as in turtles. When dry finish in same manner as a turtle.

In large lizards a light covering of compo. No. II may be employed over a hard wrapped {80} core, but is not so satisfactory as dry mounting as the skins of lizards are water-proof and consequently do not allow of moisture evaporating. With care in application the first mentioned method may be employed upon nearly all lizard specimens with most satisfactory results.

Alligators may be mounted with wrapped legs and tail and stuffed body, like the small mammal method with the exception of the head.

Be sure to remove all the jaw meat, tongue, and eye socket fat from the skulls of lizard specimens. Replace tongue and other tissues with colored wax and cotton when mouth is opened.

PREPARING AND MOUNTING A SMALL CRUSTACEAN

A crawfish or "land crab" will serve as a typical medium for describing the method of preparing specimens of this nature.

When possible, take notes of the living colors.

Crustaceans may be killed most handily with chloroform. Place the specimen in a large mouthed bottle or other vessel that may be closed tightly. Pour a little chloroform upon{81} a wad of cotton and drop it into the vessel with the specimen and close up tightly.

When beginning work, lay the specimen upon its back and with a sharp scalpel loosen the large thorax plate around its edge and remove it carefully with head and antennae left attached intact.

Separate tail entire from body meat. Split it along fleshy under side and remove muscles from it with the scalpel.

The legs will come apart and must be kept in natural order. If the claws are large and meaty, cut a round hole in under side of thick part and scrape meat out. Apply arsenic-water to all inner surfaces.

Cut wires of suitable size for all the legs. Have them enough longer than the legs so that a sharpened end will protrude to run through and clinch in the body core. Push wires in full length of legs. (Fig. 30. shows the details of making the body core of fine excelsior.) Make the core of a size to fit a little loosely into shell of body and tail.

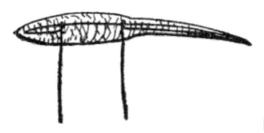

Fig. 30.

{82}

Set legs upon core as shown in Fig. 31. When the legs are properly anchored, cover the core with enough of compo. No. I. so it will fit snugly into thorax and tail shells. Place these upon the core now and press them accurately into position.

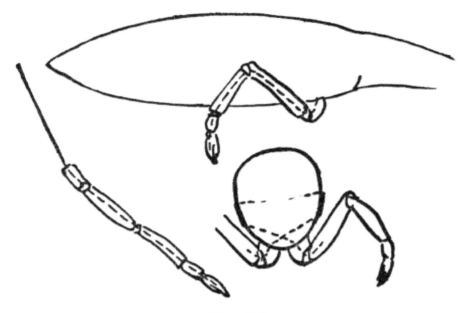

Fig. 31.

Whatever compo. squeezes out may be removed with a bit of damp cloth or sponge. Position legs and tail approximately and wire upon the base. Set the legs in their permanent position, spread or close the tail fan as desired, arrange the antennae, and set the specimen in a well ventilated spot to dry. Tint with oil colors, thinned with kerosene as they are used, laying the tints on with soft brushes.

Sanded or graveled board bases may be{83} made for birds, turtles, etc., by applying a coat of heavy shellac to top and sides of pieces, cut to required sizes and shapes, and before the shellac has a chance to dry, throwing sand or fine gravel on forcibly or laying the boards in the sand and piling sand over the moist tops, letting them lay a few moments before removing and shaking off the loose sand. Allow such bases to dry thoroughly before using.

PREPARING AND MOUNTING A VIRGINIA DEER HEAD

{87}

CHAPTER V

PREPARING AND MOUNTING A VIRGINIA DEER HEAD

Well mounted trophies of the chase are a source of delight to the fortunate sportsman who possesses them.

Antlered game heads that are mounted true to life in form and expression may go far to beautify many dining rooms, dens, and hallways, enhancing the artistic tone of the rooms in which they are well placed.

As in all taxidermy work, outline sketches direct from the fresh specimen, top and side views, both before and after skinning, are of great value in mounting deer heads.

As in other specimens, deer scalps for mounting should be as fresh as possible. If a scalp is to be kept for some little time before mounting it should be well salted.

Roll the scalp up and lay over night to drain. Next day scrape off the first salt and rub in another thorough salting. Keep the skin rolled up to prevent drying hard until mounting or sent to the tanner.{88}

An ideal deer scalp includes the neck skin entire to swell of shoulders and brisket. The incisions to be made for removing a deer scalp are shown in Fig. 32. A good sharp knife will be required for peeling the skin from the neck.

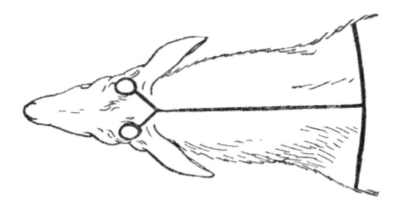

Fig. 32.

Cut very carefully up under rim of horn bases when removing skin from around them, using care not to haggle edge of skin. Use same care in skinning out the face, splitting lips and eyelids and skinning out the ears as in small mammal specimen. Remove the ear cartilages entire, after skinning their backs, beginning at the thick top edge and proceeding very carefully, looking out not to tear open the edges.

Scalps may be mounted raw or tanned. The ideal way is to use a tanned, thin pared scalp, mounting it with papier mache upon a modeled mannikin. The raw skin method is perhaps {89} easiest of application, but in all ways is not as satisfactory as the tanned skin method.

For mounting a deer scalp raw, if salted, soak out the salt by squeezing through two or three baths of cold, weak carbolic water. Dry the scalp thoroughly in fine sawdust, rubbing it into the hair and repeatedly shaking until all moisture is removed.

With a small, hardwood paring "beam," shown in <u>Fig. 33</u>, clamped to edge of table, and a sharp paring knife, remove all flesh from inner surface of skin and peel out nose cartilage. Leave nearly an inch of nostril lining around the openings.

Fig. 33.

Pare all flesh from lips, leaving a half or three-quarters inch of the lining all around them. Split white eyelid lining free to edge and leave a quarter inch of it all around the{90} openings. When skinning out the ears keep the cartilages for models.

Poison all inner surfaces of the cleaned skin with arsenic water brushed in well. Fold face, wrong side out, back upon neck. Fold neck skin flesh to flesh over face, roll the scalp up, hair side out, and lay aside in cool place over one night before mounting. The mannikin should be prepared in time so that the skin will not have to lay wet for more than a day before mounting.

It is well to prepare mannikin before skin is poisoned so that skin may be used for fitting unless accurate outline studies are at hand. With these the fitting is not necessary.

For raw-mounting the head, clean skull by boiling in a deep pail until meat comes off easily. A little washing soda in the water will help clean the bone. With a saw, cut through under side of brain cavity, lengthwise on each side of axis bone. Cut the loosened piece out with a chisel and remove brain.

Set the skull upon neck-board of suitable length (refer to studies) mounted with screws upon a cut out neck base-board of inch thick wood, as shown in Fig. 34. Fasten skull to top of neck board with nails driven through holes drilled through the bone. If turned{91} head is desired, make opening in under side of brain cavity wider and nail skull at any desired angle upon top of neck board. Screw upon back of neck base-board a one by three inch piece with free end dropping a few inches below bottom of base-board so that head may be handily set in a vise. This will allow you to get all around it and the vise will hold it at any angle, making sewing, etc., easier.

Fig. 34.

Upon skull, for jaw muscles, and upon neck board wrap excelsior, packing it hard as you go along, to required natural size. A raw skin will settle better in drying if neck is slightly smaller than natural size.

To aid in wrapping close and firm to edge of neck base-board, drive a row of small, broad{92} headed nails half into the edge, two or three inches apart all around and loop the winding-cord over these as the wrapping proceeds. Drive these nails down when wrapping is completed. (See Fig. 35 for finished wrapped excelsior head, ready for the skin.)

Fig. 35.

Drop the dry ear cartilages into warm water. In this they will quickly regain their natural shape. Using them as models make a pair of duplicates of them of thin sheet lead which may be procured from a plumber or hardware dealer. Split into the base of the cartilage so it may be spread as nearly flat as possible and lay on the lead, drawing around its outline with a nail point. Cut out the lead ears with a pair of metal-shears. Hammer into natural concave shape with a bit of heavy wood rounded into a ball at one end for the purpose. (For details of ear making see Fig. 36). {93}

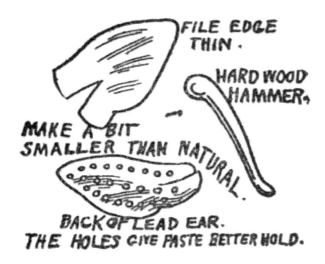

Fig. 36.

With the skin and mannikin in readiness make up a batch of plaster of paris in thin glue water, only enough glue stirred in so that it can barely be felt when the fingers are rubbed together in the water. This should retard the plaster setting for from four to six hours and give ample time for finishing the deer's face. This compo. will set immediately if used in a skin that has been treated with formaldehyde, sulphuric acid, or alum, as the glue becomes tanned and impotent by them.

Make this compo. thick and stiff and mix into it some chopped manila fiber. For finishing one deer face and ear-butts about a quart and a half of the compo. should be made. This should cover the face thinly, fill the ear-butts, set the eyes, and fill nose and mouth details out.

In beginning the setting of the scalp into {94} place, cover the lead ears thinly with the compo. and slip them into the ear skins. The lead will have to be partly folded together to accomplish this and spread again when inside. If edges of ears have been torn open in skinning, sew them up neatly from the outside, using a small round needle and small thread before the lead is placed.

With the cartilages set, fill the ear butts with compo., squeezing it out upon the lead a little way that it may brace the ears when set finally.

Set the mannikin in the vise for convenience. Cover skull with a thin layer of compo. where bone is exposed and slip the face skin into place. Hold the scalp up now by tying a heavy cord under the jaw and behind the horns. Draw the neck skin into place and tie it up with a piece of cord about the neck near base. Now, for better convenience in sewing, remove the head from the vise, set front of neck base on the floor and lean the antlers against a chair seat, back of neck up. Draw corners of antler cuts together back of the horns.

Begin at one horn and sew to joint of the Y cut. Sew from the other horn and then continue down the neck to the base, using medium stitches and drawing tight. This method of{95} sewing a game head is the only exception, in taxidermy, to sewing toward the head. For a raw scalp use a sail needle and waxed ends. For a tanned scalp, a large fur needle and strong linen.

With the sewing completed, turn to nailing the scalp to the back-board. Turn the free edge of skin down over back of board and nail firmly with short broad headed nails so that when the surplus is trimmed off a turned over edge of skin two or three inches wide will remain, held snugly by nails set two inches apart. Count upon finishing a raw head all up at one go when using the plaster compo. This is the only compo. which can be recommended to hold raw, haired skins down, as the material must set before the skin begins to dry and pull.

Before turning to finishing the face, unscrew the holding piece from back of neck-board and nail up the part of skin's edge that it covered. Replace the piece and set head in vise facing you. Pinch and mold the ear skin tightly upon the compo. covered lead and model the ear-butts into shape firmly against the head.

Run a strong-threaded fur needle, with large knot at end of thread, through middle of upper edge of each lead ear. Draw ears up to desired position and wrap thread around a{96} convenient part of antlers to hold until compo. sets. Next loop a cord under each ear at base of cartilage and tie over antlers to hold lower end of cartilage from sagging until set. When ears are finished, press face skin into compo. upon skull and massage it down to hold firmly.

Fill eyelids thinly inside flap of lining, place a little compo. in hollow of sockets, and set eyes.

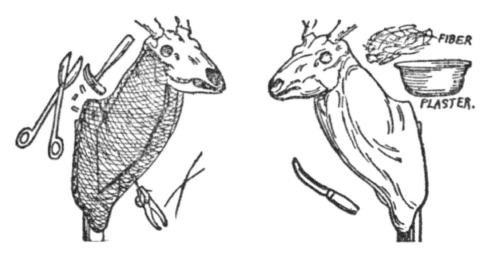

Fig. 37.

Deer are usually quite fleshy just over the eyes. Place this filling before eyes are set. Also press a little compo. into the hollows of the suborbital glands and with the fingers work these fleshy eye details out roughly and finish with a modeling tool, pressing the slits of suborbital glands in deeply with a thick-edged instrument. See that the face skin is worked{97} down firmly and smoothly clear to the nose.

Fill nose and upper lip and model them into natural shape. Lastly, fill chin and lower lip. Tuck lower lip up well under upper and model lips and chin into proper relation to each other.

If any compo. has gotten into the hair wipe it out with a damp sponge. Leave head in the vise until compo. is set and then hang in a well ventilated place to dry. Do not hang near stove or radiator.

When thoroughly dried out, brush dust out of hair and finish the eyelids, nostrils, etc., with wax and cotton, burned in, same as given for finishing a small mammal.

If placing the head upon a shield, use at least four strong screws of a length to go nearly through the two boards.

For mounting a deer scalp tanned, the preparation is very different. Scalps may be had tanned at a number of reputable fur houses throughout the country at a small cost. To get best results, send scalps and rug-skins in to the tanner with ears skinned out and eyelids and lips split and nose cartilage pared out. Tanned scalps, if kept from moths, may be preserved unmounted for a long time.

When required for mounting, a tanned scalp need only be relaxed with water brushed or{98} sponged into the flesh side and, when soft, poisoned with arsenic-water and folded together, flesh to flesh, over one night.

The process of mounting a tanned scalp differs from the raw in that it is set up on a wire and plaster shell, more carefully shaped than the excelsior form. The entire scalp is stuck down to the shell with compo. No. I rubbed well into the skin and upon the shell. The face and ears are set and finished with compo. No. II, which, as before stated, is No. I thickened to the consistency of modeling clay with plaster of paris. This method gives much finer and more permanent results.

For details of plaster and wire mannikin, see Fig. 37. This type of shell is made as follows: Set the cleaned skull upon neck-board and back-board same as for wrapping excelsior neck.

Half-inch mesh chicken wire will do, if no free mesh wire can be procured, for building the frame. The wire neck is best placed in halves. The shaping will require considerable cutting and neat manipulation with pincers and hammer and tying with bits of wire. Use staple tacks to fasten wire to edge of back-board. The wire shell should be smaller than natural neck to allow for coat of plaster and fiber. For this make up not more than half{99} a wash basin at a time, mixing the plaster with plain water in the ordinary way. Make the batches middling thick, enough so that it will not drizzle from the wire.

Pick a quantity of fiber into small handfuls. To apply, dip a film of the manila fiber into the plaster, drag it out over edge of dish to remove surplus plaster, and apply to wire shell. Work fast enough to keep ahead of plaster setting. Wipe each application out smooth as you go. Apply a thin coat, very smooth, all over the skull and model on the jaw muscles with the plaster and fiber.

When plaster is set, surface the shell and remove all inequalities by paring with an ordinary small butcher-knife. Allow to thoroughly dry and apply a good coat of medium thin shellac.

Have this type of mannikin completed, dried, and shellaced before moistening and preparing the tanned skin.

To prepare mammal skins in the field, for transportation and keeping, remove skins carefully, same as for immediate mounting. Salt thoroughly, rubbing in well, and roll up to drain over night. Next day shake out the first salt, which will be found saturated with juices, rub fresh salt in all over, and roll up over another night. In this condition small skins{100} may be sealed in glass jars or friction top tins and kept damp thus for some time.

To make a preserving "pickle" for keeping skins wet, boil salt in water until heaviest brine possible to make is produced. Add a tablespoonful of carbolic acid to the gallon while hot. Stir well. Let the solution cool thoroughly before submerging skins in it.

Skins should always be put through the double dry salting before going into "pickle." Keep in covered earthen jars.

For making up into rugs, send animal skins to a good tanner, first skinning out the ears and paring out lips and nose.

To make an open-mouthed rug head, use the natural skull when possible. Set the jaws open solidly with plaster of paris and at the same time lay a plaster core between lower jaw for the artificial tongue. Set the skull upon a cut-out base-board as shown in Fig. 38.

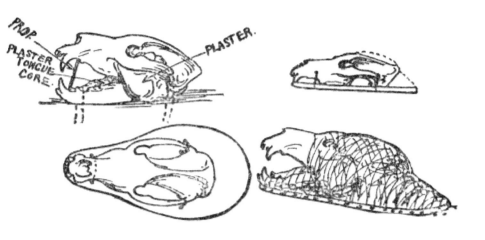

Fig. 38.

{101}

Drive nails half in all around back and side edges of this base-board and wrap on filling of excelsior for jaws and flare of neck. Drive the nails down tight after wrapping is completed.

Mount the head before stretching the skin. Relax the head with water and poison same as deer scalp.

Use plaster and glue-water compo. as in raw deer scalp. If a snarling expression is desired, model the wrinkles on the muzzle with an edged wooden tool. Tuck the lip lining well under the filling, so they will hold in place when the plaster is set. Finish details of face same as in other mounting.

Finish the tongue and gums by melting colored wax and cotton upon core and bone with hot iron, modeling and carving to shape when cool. After the head is mounted and set, stretch the skin. Moisten the flesh side to soften it up well.

Nail down the rear end upon floor to its widest spread, with hind legs pointing back on a slight slant. Draw the skin forward and spread forelegs and front end to widest extent and nail down in accurate line with hind part. Now work from side to side, nailing skin out to its widest extent and in symmetrical lines. Always stretch a rug-skin hair side down. A{102} slight wash of arsenic-water may be applied after the skin is stretched and while yet moist, care being used not to mess the hair with the solution.

When dry, the skin is ready to line. Lay the felt lining upon the floor and the skin upon it and cut around the skin, allowing three or four inches for pinked edge.

With a pinking iron cut scalloped edge and enough of a narrow strip to gather fully all around just inside the outer edge. Lay skin on lining and mark its edge with tailor's chalk. Sew the gathered edge just inside this chalk mark so that the stitch will be covered by the skin.

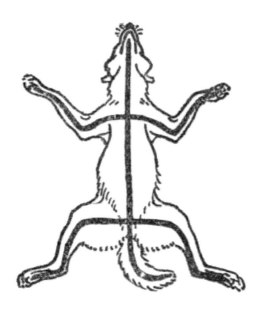

Fig. 39.

Quilt skin upon the lining with a good layer of cotton wadding between. Be sure and not{103} draw down a bunch of hair under each loop. Tie the knots neatly on under side.

Fig. 39 shows incisions to make in removing a pelt for a symmetrical rug. Rug skins are best dried with no preservative whatever. In drying skins, stretch them symmetrically and dry in the shade.

{105}

PREPARING AND MOUNTING A COYOTE

{107}

CHAPTER VI

PREPARING AND MOUNTING A COYOTE

73

This method may be applied to specimens from the size of a red fox or a bobcat up to a timber wolf. Remove the skin and prepare it in same way as that of a small mammal for mounting. When the carcass is bared in skinning, measure the girth of the neck at middle and at base; of the chest just behind the forelegs; the abdomen at its middle; the upper-arm at middle; the forearm just below elbow; the thigh at middle; the shank just below swell of thigh muscles back of knee, and the tail near its base. (See Fig. 40 for measurements.)

Lay the carcass upon a large piece of wrapping paper and take an outline of it complete, both before and after skinning.

Use same incisions and remove skin identically as in small specimen. Upon the outline sketch of peeled complete carcass set down the girth measurements in their proper places as taken with the tape. As in smaller specimens, {108} these outline sketches will be found of great value as an aid to preserving natural lines in mounting.

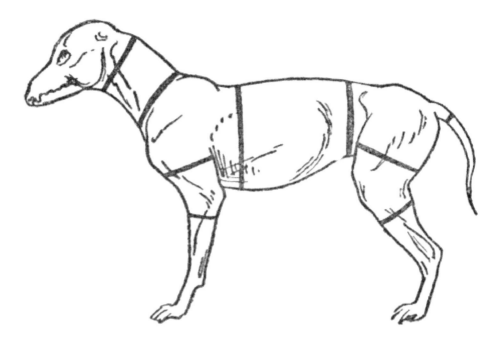

Fig. 40.

Wire the leg bones same as in a small mammal, using soft iron rod of sufficient size to support the specimen firmly. In our coyote a quarter-inch rod will be required. In a bobcat a three-sixteenths-inch rod will be large enough to support sturdily.

Bend the leg rods to fit the joints in position desired. Cut the rods of a length so that six or eight inches will protrude from the feet and eight or ten inches will remain free above to anchor to the body core. Bind the rods to the{109} leg-bones with strong, light cord, doing the firmest wrapping near the joints.

Working over the body outline, cut a one-inch-thick board core that will set well within the outline. (See Fig. 41.)

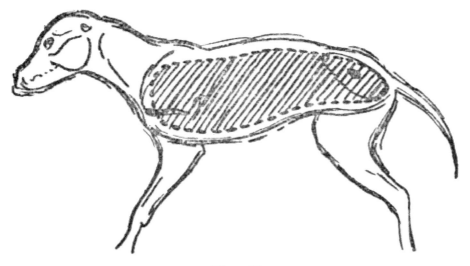

Fig. 41.

Cut a neck-rod of same size as for legs, having it twice as long as neck and head. Near one end of the neck-rod bend a jog to hold well when set with plaster of paris and chopped fiber into the brain cavity of the cleaned skull.

Wrap the leg muscles upon the bones same as in a small specimen, except pull the excelsior rather smooth for the purpose instead of rolling it in the palms. Make the Achilles tendon in same way and leave back of thigh off to be stuffed.

When the plaster to hold neck-rod in head{110} is set, anchor the skull by the rod to the core-board in proper relation to the body. To do this, run the rod through a hole drilled through the board, clinch rod down forward and back with a hammer on anvil or vise, and fasten with staples, or drill a small hole through core-board each side of rod and tie the rod down with a strong loop of wire twisted down with the pliers.

Wrap the skull muscles on with excelsior rolled in palms of hands. Wrap a tail of pulled excelsior laid straight along a wire much smaller than is used in legs.

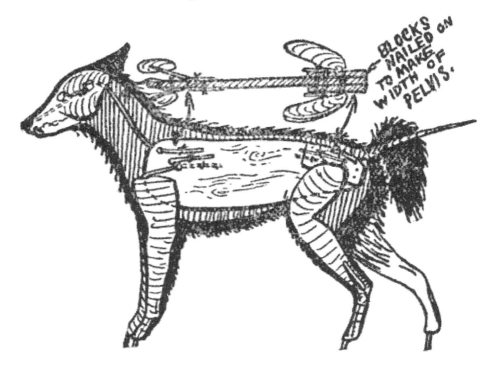

Fig. 42.

Drill the center-board for legs and tail as shown in Fig. 42, which shows general assembling{111} details. When the legs, head, and tail are finished, push the head and body-core into place in the skin, shove in the legs and tail, and wire the legs and tail fast in the center-board same as head was fastened.

The remainder of the mounting is accomplished in exactly the same way as the filling and finishing of a small mammal specimen, *i. e.*, by stuffing the neck, body, and back of thighs and finishing the face and feet with a batch of papier-mache compo.

No. 2. If the mouth is to be open, follow directions given for finishing an entire rug-head.

Fig. 43.

To hold in the hollow of the flanks, cut several short, strong pieces of wire, sharpen{112} them to cutting points, push them through the skin along line of hollow in front of hip, drive them firmly into the core-board, and then, with cutting pliers clinch their ends down to hold the skin in and cut off surplus wire, picking the fur out well to cover them. (See Fig. 43.)

Fig. 44.

To support the compo.-filled ears until set and dry, drive a sharpened wire into the head, through hollow of ear. Point the wire in direction ear is to lay or stand and between ear and wire lay a loose, flat wad of cotton or tow. With a furrier's needle and thread take a narrow loop through center of ear near tip and tie{113} lightly around wire to hold until dry. When dry remove the thread with scissors and the wires by a slight twist with pliers.

Mammals of the sizes named may be mounted so skillfully by this method that they cannot be told from mannikin specimens.

Specimens of this size need not be entirely mounted at one sitting. Prepare the skin, wire and wrap the legs and head, and make the center-board in one day, assemble the specimen and place the body filling the next day, and make the feet, mount the specimen, and finish the head the third day.

A little carbolic acid in the arsenic-water will help keep the skin from slipping the hair. Also keep unfinished parts wrapped in damp cloths wrung from carbolic acid water.

Printed in Great Britain
by Amazon